Grid Poems

A Guide and Workbook

James P. Wagner (Ishwa)

Grid Poems

Table of Contents

What Is A Grid Poem?

One day I was sitting a lounge I frequent readings through several books about the history of the sonnet. I was preparing for a presentation I was giving and wanted to brush up on my knowledge of international sonneteers. While reading I came across a description of one poetry book that blew my mind. It's called *Cent mille milliards de poèmes* is a book by Raymond Queneau a French Poet.

The title translates to "One Hundred Million Million Poems." The funny thing is, the book only contains 10 sonnets. Yet it each sonnet is written in a specific way--each line is on a card you can punch out and rearrange the order. The lines all have the same rhyme scheme and the same sounds, and can be rearranged into different combinations numbering $10^{14.}$

All that from 10 sonnets. I was dumbfounded, and also inspired. It got me thinking of various other poetic exercises and forms I had seen over the years, and how in certain workshops I have led, the advice I have given many poets countless times was "simply switch the order of the lines" and we would all be amazed how much improved the poem would be, with the same words, in different order.

So on a spur of the moment impulsive challenge to myself, I put down the book I was reading, turned to one of my writing notebooks and decided to see if I could write a poem to be read across and down. I found this hard to do without putting extra separation on the words, so I drew myself a little grid. It was 5 by 5. This is how the Grid Poem as you are going to read about in this text, came to be.

On the next page you are going to see an example of the "Grid Poem" in its grid form.

Read Across, Then Down

The	Reflection	Of	The	Water(')s
Images	Brings	An	Immersion	That
Present(s)	An	Eerie	Sight	Beheld
Memory's	Eternal	Mirror	Shows	History
Ghosts	Chase	Shadow('s)	Past	Lessons

You might notice a few things when looking at this Grid. First and foremost, how much can be gotten from a mere 25 words.

You might also notice the parenthesis that allow for double-use possessives, and that there can be frequent enjambments.

Now take a look at the poems in actual poetic form, without the grid.

Across:

The reflection of the water
Images bring an immersion that
Presents The reflection of the water
Memory's eternal mirror shows history
Ghosts chase shadow's past lessons

Down:

The images present memory's ghosts
Reflection brings an eternal chase
Of an eerie mirror shadow
The immersion sight shows past
Water that beheld history lessons.

So here you see that from this simple 25 word grid, we have gotten arguably two complete poems. One can play around with the possessives and the punctuation as they want to, but the essence is, the same words, presented differently, bring about entirely different poems. And while this concept is generally obvious, the grid really helps to bring it into focus and get the creative energies flowing.

How To Write A Grid Poem

Writing a Grid Poem can be a little tricky at first but the basic structure is easy enough to learn. As you probably guessed from the example previous, it starts with mapping out a grid, either in a notebook by hand, or in your word processor.

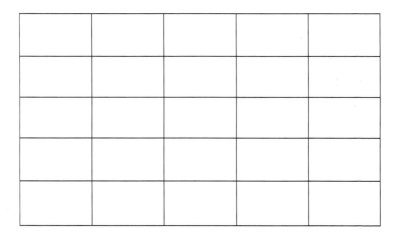

For my purposes and what I've personally found best to work with myself is the 5 by 5 grid to create a poem of 25 words.

Of course, a 5 by 5 grid isn't the only size grid you can do.

One could give a shot at a 3 x 3 grid if the idea of a 5 x 5 is too much. Think of it as a grid haiku (haikai.)

I	Am	Lost(,)
Am	Deciding	I'm
Sure	What	Spent

Across:

I Am Lost
Am Deciding I'm
Sure What Spent

Down:

I Am Sure
Am Deciding What
Lost, I'm Spent

7

With fewer words there are fewer options, and so punctuation might become more important as you can see with the comma that works one way (but not the other.)

But as you can see, there are possibilities with a 3 x 3 poem.

Of course, smaller is not the only way one can go, if one is brave enough they can try for a larger grid.

Want to try this grid? Good luck. I don't really want to try it myself! But I'm sure there are some poets out there who would like the challenge.

So let's assume one is going to start and try with the standard 5 x 5 grid. How does one get started?

First draw yourself the grid:

Once you have the grid set up, it helps to decide on a few words you want to make sure go in the poem. If you are working with a writing group or doing a challenge, you can decide the word bank together. If you are doing it solo, you can decide the words to be anchors of the poem.

- Divine
- Destiny
- Sacrifice
- Patience
- Enlightened

So let's say these 5 words were the word bank? For a 25 word poem or 5 x 5 about 5 words is what you want to start. Then plug them into the grid to start.

	Divine			
Destiny				
				Patience
Enlightened		Sacrifice		

The	*Divine*	Offer	A	Page
Destiny	Speaks	By	Voice	Illuminated
Of	Purpose	God	Commands	*Patience*
Faith	Accepts(,)	Delays(,)	Praying(,)	Paused(.)
Enlightened	Follow(s)	*Sacrifice(,)*	Penitence	Waiting.

And as you can see once they are plugged in, you can add the rest of the words to complete the poem.

- You can have alternative possessives and enjambments

- Try to use words in their base form as much as possible

- You CAN use the same word twice in cases of conjunctions but try to limit this.

- Pick certain words you want to include and be flexible with the rest.

- Reorganizing the position of words in the grid is probable. It might take a few times to get it.

A "Grid Poem " doesn't necessarily need to produce complete poems on its own as much as be a worthy exercise to give ideas. You can find while looking through the words in the grid many different lines that could be transposed into other poems you are writing, or perhaps function as prompts for poems.

The	**Reflection**	**Of**	*The*	Water(')s
Images	Brings	**An**	*Immersion*	That
Present(s)	An	**Eerie**	Sight	*Beheld*
Memory's	<u>Eternal</u>	**Mirror**	Shows	*History*
<u>Ghosts</u>	<u>Chase</u>	<u>Shadow('s)</u>	Past	*Lessons*

Take a look at the words that stick out here in bold:

The Reflection Of An Eerie Mirror

Sounds like a good verse to put in a poem, no?

How about the underlined words?

<u>Ghosts Chase Eternal Shadows</u>

And the italicized words?

The Immersion Beheld History Lessons

Any one of these lines could be a verse in another poem. They could be the first lines of entire other poems, or the finishing line of other poems. But as you look at the grid, different patterns of the words, in different orders will stick out and give ideas and inspiration.

So even if your attempt at a grid poem doesn't produce a complete poem across and down, there is still plenty of value to be had in the exercise.

Grid Poem Examples

Since introducing the grid poem I've used it as a prompt and exercise in many workshop type settings. Some of the poets who attend have really taken to the form. And so, in this section we'll be taking a look at some of the creative ways a few other poets have used the form.

Jim Landwher

Before	Lies	Spilling	Magic(.)	Nuance(.)
The	Water	Over	Death's	Unwelcome
Entrance	Running	Monochrome	Image(s)	Morphing
To	Melancholy	Filled	Enchanted	Ghosts
Happiness	And	Divine	Beyond	Imagination

Across

Before lies spilling magic nuance
the water over death's unwelcome entrance
running monochrome images,
morphing to melancholy filled enchanted ghosts.
Happiness and divine beyond imagination

Down

Before the entrance to happiness
lies water running melancholy and
spilling over monochrome filled divine magic.
Death's images enchanted beyond nuance.
Unwelcome morphing ghosts imagination

Jim Landwher used the grid to a T and as a result got two complete poems across and down. He used a lot of the tools we talked about, such as punctuation or plurals in parenthesis to indicate usage in one direction but not the other. And when reading the poems in their solo form, you can see the usage of that in action.

<u>Cathy Hailey</u>

Water	Pool(')s	Around	Creek	Crossing(.)
Root	Reflection	Twists,	Sparking	Light(.)
Flashes	Create(s)	Tap	Rhythm	Ripples(,)
Dance	Mirage	Manifested	Into	Music(.)
Dream(.)	Forest(.)	Crescendo,	Truth(.)	Alive.

Across

Water pools around creek crossing
Root reflection twists sparking light
Flashes create tap rhythm ripples
Dance mirage manifested into music
Dream forest crescendo truth alive.

Down

Water root flashes dance dream
Pools reflection create mirage forest
Around twists tap manifested crescendo
Creek sparking rhythm into truth
Cross light ripples music alive.

Mary Langer Thompson

erendipitous	Highways	Illuminate	Mirage	Lakes(,)
ntrance	As	Portal	Of	Protest
hrough	Images(,.)	Miracle(')s	Clarity	Swirling(,)
orlds	Travel(.)	Rivers	bend	Lonesome(.)
ultitudinous(,)	mercies	Calm(.)	Morning(.)	Fog.

21

Across

Serendipitous highways illuminate mirage lakes,
entrance as portal of protest
through images, miracle's clarity swirling
worlds travel. Rivers bend lonesome.
Multitudinous mercies calm morning fog.

Down

Serendipitous entrance through worlds multitudinous,
highways as images. Travel mercies
illuminate portal miracles, rivers calm.
Mirage of clarity bends morning.
Lakes protest swirling, lonesome fog.

Mary's grid poem makes very good use of punctuation. Take a look in the second column, third row for the word Images.

Images(,.) see the double punctuation she has here? It indicates that in the across version of the poem, a comma follows images, whereas in the down version of the poem, a period follows.

This type of double-grammatical usage in the grid set up reminds us that when writing, the words can be the same, but the punctuation, or the inflection, the pause, all these nuances can have a profound effect on the meaning of the words. We all know this inherently, but sometimes it is easy to forget. One of the benefits of the grid exercise is a reminder to remember what we already know.

Mike Vreeland

Nature	calling	softly	for	safety
green	**Forest**	whispers	loving	knowle
and	spirits	**Dreams (s)**	universal	truth
Water	flowing	toward	**Destiny**	and
blue	future	peace	through	**Music**

Across

Nature calling softly for safety,
Green forest whispers loving knowledge,
and spirits dream universal truth:
Water flowing toward destiny and
blue future peace through music.

Down

Nature green and water blue
calling forest spirits flowing future
softly whispers dreams toward peace
for loving universal destiny through
safety, knowledge, truth and music.

Alex Edwards-Bourdrez

Water(s)	their	mirages	with	music
pour	laughter	through	echoing	canyons
sparkles	and	river(s)	flood(s)	boulders
in	frightening	screams	within	prisons
between	dreams(s)	flowing	rapids	echo.

Across

Water their mirages with music.
Pour laughter through, echoing. Canyons
sparkle, and rivers flood boulders
in frightening screams. Within prisons,
between dreams, flowing rapids echo.

Down

Waters pour sparkles in between
their laughter, and frightening dreams—
mirages through rivers—scream, flowing
with echoing floods within rapids—
Music, canyons, boulders, prisons echo.

Katherine Gotthardt, M.Ed.

Candlelight	In	Darkened	Rooms	Reflecti
Shadows	Specters'	**Smoke**	Disappearing	Beneath
Some	**Flickering**	Phantasms	Asking	Question
Without	Answers	ways	of	**Extingu**
Fire	Without	Destroying	**Flames**	Warmth

Across

Candlelight in darkened rooms reflecting
shadows, specters' smoke disappearing beneath
some flickering phantasms asking questions
without answers, ways of extinguishing
fire without destroying flames' warmth.

Down

Candlelight shadows, some without fire,
in specters' flickering answers without
darkened smoke, phantasms' ways destroying
rooms, disappearing, asking of flames
reflecting beneath questions, extinguishing warmth.

Modified Line Breaks

Candlelight in darkened rooms,
reflecting shadows,
specters' smoke disappearing
beneath some flickering phantasms
asking questions without answers,
ways of extinguishing fire
without destroying flames' warmth.

Candlelight shadows,
some without fire,
in specters' flickering answers
without darkened smoke,
phantasms' ways destroying rooms,
disappearing, asking of flames reflecting
beneath questions,
extinguishing warmth.

With a Few Words Changed

I remember you
standing in candlelight,
darkened rooms
reflecting shadows,
specters' smoke disappearing
beneath some flickering phantasms
asking questions without answers:
What are the ways of extinguishing fire
without destroying flames' warmth?

Candlelight shadows,
some without fire.
In specters' flickering answers
without darkened smoke,
phantasms' ways are destroying rooms.
Disappearing, the dead begin
asking of the flames reflecting
beneath questions:
How can even think
of extinguishing warmth?

Notice the ingenuity in Katherine's use of the grid? Not only does she get the pure across and down poems by using it, but she goes a couple of steps further and modifies the line breaks to give a different look and feel to the poems she made...and then she takes the base of the grid poems and changes a few words to make entirely different poems.

This is perfectly in line with the general spirit of the grid poem in the sense that the across and down is not the only thing you can get out of using it. If you are creative, you can shape and form various poems from the words in your grid, and get inspiration from many different angles.

Chryssa Velissariou

Morning	Your	Face(s')	Shine(s)	Blinding
Comet	Inspiration('s)	Illusions	Amaze(s)	Me
Almost	Stopping	My	Wants	And
Faint	Thoughts(')	Empowering	No	Strength
For	Darkening	Days(')	Passion('s)	Emerge(s)

Across (Modified)

Morning!
Your face shines blinding comet
Inspiration('s) illusions amaze me
almost stopping my wants and faint thoughts' empowering
No strength for darkening days
Passion emerges

Down (Modified)

Morning comet
Almost faint for your inspiration
Stopping thoughts
Darkening faces' Illusions
My empowering days 'shine amazes wants
No passion's blinding me
And strength emerges

Rose Miller

Envious	river	water	nature's	mirror
Attempt(s)	cloud('s)	mirage	recording	images
To	reflect	metamorphosis	its	desire
Capture(s)	sepia	dusk	magic	slowly
Stars	glow	night	sky	darkens

Across

Envious river water nature's mirror
Attempt cloud's mirage recording images
To reflect metamorphosis its desire
Captures sepia dusk magic slowly
Stars glow night sky darkens

Down

Envious attempts to capture stars
River clouds reflect sepia glow
Water mirage metamorphosis dusk night
Nature's recording its magic sky
Mirror images desire slowly darkens

Elizabeth Singletary

Reflection(ive)	Ripples	Along	The	River('s)
Tides	To	Harmonized	Tunes(.)	Sung
Through	Calm	Water (.,)	Images(,)	Of
Peaceful	Folk	Entrance(d)(.)	A	Joyful
Stream(.)	Together(.)	Mount	Rising	Music

Word Bank:

Entrance
Music
Reflection
River
Water

Across:

Reflection ripples along the river's tides
To harmonized tunes sung through calm waters.
Images of peaceful folk entrance a joyful stream.
Together mount rising music.

Down:

Reflective tides through peaceful stream
Ripples to calm folk together.
Along harmonized waters, entranced.
Mount the tunes.
Images, a rising river sung of joyful music.

Notice how in this poem, the poet lists the word bank of the words they plugged into the grid from the get go. Also notice how they chose to use enjambment of the lines and different line breaks in their version of the across and down rather than use the traditional 5 lines. With grid poems, the rules are basically guidelines--as long as creativity comes from it, that is the important part.

Lynette Esposito

Empty	yellow	destiny('s)	screams	*come*
Interrupted	dusty	prayers	cry	*help*
Curved	roads	lead	to	light
Dreams	lead	to	faith's	reveal
Dance	on	blood	dark	hope

Across:

Empty yellow destiny screams *come*
interrupted dusty prayers cry *help*
curved roads lead to light
dreams lead to faith's reveal
dance on blood dark hope

Down:

Empty interrupted curved dreams dance
yellow dusty roads lead on
destiny's prayers lead to blood
screams cry to faith's dark
come help light reveal hope.

Vincent F. A. Golphin

Jazz	unmasks	as	spirit's	divine
Roots	core	unleashed	phantasm's	jetsam
Itself	desires	illuminate	hunger	reaches
In	worry's	soul	hides	distant
Dreams	prod	visions	beyond	mirages.

Across:

Jazz unmasks as spirit's divine
roots core unleashed phantasm's jetsam.
Itself, desires illuminate, hunger reaches
in worry's soul hides distant
dreams, prod visions beyond mirages.

Down:

Jazz roots itself in dreams,
unmasks core desires, worries, prod,
as unleashed, illuminate soul visions.
Spirit's phantasm's hunger hides beyond.
Divine jetsam reaches distant mirages.

<u>Tanya Adèle Koehnke</u>

Jack-in-the-Box

Tin	toy	wind-up	crank	plays
carnival	melodies.	Confettied	metal	cube
bursts	Surprise!	**Jack_in_the_Box**	pops	up!
Lid	closes.	Floppy	puppet	on
a	spring	folds	into	darkness.

Across:

Tin toy wind-up crank plays
carnival melodies. Confettied metal cube
bursts Surprise! **Jack-in-the-Box** pops up!
Lid closes. Floppy puppet on
a spring folds into darkness.

Down:

Tin carnival bursts Lid a
toy melodies. Surprise! closes. spring
wind-up Confettied **Jack-in-the-Box** floppy folds
crank metal pops puppet into
plays cube up! on darkness.

Notice how Tanya has Jack-in-the-Box strategically placed in
the center box so it is the center word in the poem either way.
Popping out in a poetic metaphor to the toy itself. With the
poem centered like above, you can see the center word stick
out more.

Grid Poem Workbook

Now that you know what a grid poem is, and you've seen several examples of both the traditional and several non-traditional ways to do them, your turn to start writing grid poems! In the following pages, we have grids lined out, for the typical 5 x 5, 25 word grid poem for you to use as a template. In some of them we will provide word banks, in others we will have suggested words plugged in, and others will be entirely blank for you to do what you want with.

Good luck as you venture into the creation of this unique and exciting form, hopefully it will inspire you and you will get some good poems or at least good verse out of it.

As a bonus, get together with some friends or a workshop group and do some grid poems together. A fun exercise if the group is small enough (3-7 people) is to each pick a word to fit somewhere in the grid. Try it out and see how it goes.

Word Bank: (Choose any 3)

Metaphor
Asteroid
Wish
Appear
Vanish
Lament
Dance

Word Bank (Choose Any 4)

Surprise
Divine
Scream
Lofty
Ambition
Creation
Replicate
Learn

Word Bank (Choose Any 5)

Real

Illusion

Resent

Addiction

Desire

Crossing

Perpetuate

Resist

Spirit

Word Bank (Use All 3 Anywhere)

Commitment

Docile

Erratic

Shining				
	Message			
				Miracle

Word Bank (Already Placed)

Shining
Message
Miracle

Free Grid

Write some words to possibly use in it below.

_____   _____

_____   _____

_____   _____

_____   _____

Free Grid

Write some words to possibly use in it below.

_____   _____

_____   _____

_____   _____

_____   _____

Free Grid

Write some words to possibly use in it below.

_____   _____

_____   _____

_____   _____

_____   _____

Free Grid

Write some words to possibly use in it below.

_____	_____
_____	_____
_____	_____
_____	_____

Free Grid

Write some words to possibly use in it below.

_____   _____

_____   _____

_____   _____

_____   _____

Free Grid

Write some words to possibly use in it below.

_____   _____

_____   _____

_____   _____

_____   _____

About the Author

James P. Wagner (Ishwa) is an editor, publisher, award-winning fiction writer, essayist, historian performance poet, and alum twice over (BA & MALS) of Dowling College. He is the publisher for Local Gems Poetry Press and the Senior Founder and President of the Bards Initiative. He is also the founder and Grand Laureate of Bards Against Hunger, a series of poetry readings and anthologies dedicated to gathering food for local pantries that operates in over a dozen states. His most recent individual collection of poetry is *Everyday Alchemy*. He was the Long Island, NY National Beat Poet Laureate from 2017-2019. He was the Walt Whitman Bicentennial Convention Chairman and teaches poetry workshops at the Walt Whitman Birthplace State Historic Site. James has edited over 60 poetry anthologies and hosted book launch events up and down the East Coast. He was named the National Beat Poet Laureate of the United States from 2020-2021.

Made in the USA
Middletown, DE
24 June 2021

42713423R00035